Fearon Teacher Aids, a division of **David S. Lake Publishers**

Playing with Logic

Mark Schoenfield
and
Jeannette Rosenblatt

Reproducible activities for grades 3-5

For Helen and Roy

Editorial director: Ina Tabibian
Editor: Ronald Scro
Managing editor: Claire Connelly
Cover and interior design: Walt Shelly
Illustrations: Walt Shelly, Bob Morrison
Design director: Eleanor Mennick
Production editor: Stephen Feinstein
Manufacturing director: Casimira Kostecki

ISBN-0-8224-5310-X

Printed in the United States of America

1. 9 8 7 6 5 4 3 2 1

CONTENTS

INTRODUCTION

Third, fourth and fifth graders love to play games—cards, board games, and of course, video games. This natural love for games and strategies can be applied to logical puzzles, and students can begin to sharpen the logical skills they may not realize they have. The purpose of this book is to bring children to a greater awareness of the powers their minds possess and of the ways they can use logical reasoning to solve problems.

The activities in this book are divided into five categories. The first is *relationships,* which involves classifying and comparing shapes and ideas. The next three are *sequencing, inference,* and *deduction.* The final section, *group activities,* is a collection of logical games for the entire class to play. These games use the skills developed in the previous sections.

Each section begins with an introduction to the skills practiced in that section and suggests a few discussion ideas. The activities can be worked through systematically, but this is not necessary. Students who have completed other classwork can perform the activities independently, or you can distribute the worksheets for a change in class routine. The activities take about ten or fifteen minutes each.

The answer key is in the last few pages of the book. The students may want to compare and discuss their answers before comparing them with the key.

RELATIONSHIPS

The ability to recognize how objects, shapes, and words are related is a basic logical skill.

Make a Set I and II: Students will classify objects by locations and uses. By eliminating the object that does not belong with the others and then completing the sentence which follows it, students will define a set. In class discussions, students can add elements to the sets or make up their own sets. They will discover that sometimes a group of objects might fit into more than one set. You might list a few words that begin with the same letter or that have the same number of syllables. Then have students guess other words in the set until they figure out how the set is defined.

The Zoo on Planet Woo and Creatures of the Lost Island: Students will follow rules to fit objects into sets. In class discussion, students can expand the sets by drawing their own animals, or they can make up their own classification rules. A class discussion after each activity will help students who were confused by one activity to successfully complete the next activity.

Shapes Alike and Shapes Relate: Students will exercise visual discrimination. They will recognize how two shapes are related and apply this relationship to other shapes. The first few should be worked out in front of the class.

Animalogies I, II, and III: Students will combine discrimination skills with basic knowledge of animals. The third activity allows the student to creatively exercise logic.

Make a Set I

Each *set* below has four objects. Three of the objects are often found in the same place. Cross out the object that does not belong. Then choose a phrase from the list at the bottom of the page to complete the sentence above each *set* of objects.

1. These three are found _____ .

2. These three are found _____ .

3. These three are found _____ .

4. These three are found _____ .

a. in a toolbox   b. at a shoestore   c. in an office
d. at a school   e. in a kitchen   f. at the beach

Name _____   3

Make a Set II

Each *set* below has four objects. Three of the objects can be used for the same purpose. Cross out the object that does not belong. Then choose a phrase from the list at the bottom of the page to complete the sentence above each *set* of objects.

1. These three are used _____ .

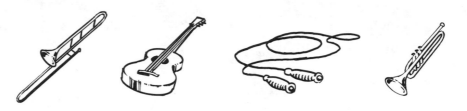

2. These three are used _____ .

3. These three are used _____ .

4. These three are used _____ .

a. for baseball   b. for traveling   c. for cooking
d. for swimming   e. for playing   f. for making music

4   Name _____

The Zoo on Planet Woo

Can you identify these rare animals from the zoo on planet Woo?
The zookeeper has identified the first one for you.

A *Scoo* is any animal that has more than two eyes.
Put a circle around all Scoos.

A *Frooch* is any animal that has at least one horn.
Put a triangle around all Frooches.

A *Ploom* is any animal that does *not* have a beard.
Put a square around all Plooms.

1.   2.   3.   4.

5.   6.   7.   8.

Just for fun, draw a Scoo Frooch Ploom on the back of this page!

Name _____

Creatures of the Lost Island

A few new animals have been discovered on the Lost Island of Maynard. You must classify them before they can be sent to zoos. Be careful—one of the animals does not fit into any of the classifications.

Only *mammals* on Maynard have whiskers.
Put a circle around the mammals.

Only *arachnids* on Maynard have eight legs.
Put a triangle around the arachnids.

Only *anuras* on Maynard do *not* have tails.
Put a square around the anuras.

1.

2.

3.

4.

5.

6.

7.

8.

9.

6   Name _____

Animalogies I

Each numbered sentence is missing one word. Choose the word that *best* completes the sentence. Then write the word in the blank space. (If you need a hint, look at the statement below the sentence.)

1. Colt is to horse as puppy is to _____.
   goat   calf   dog   fox
   (A colt is a young horse.)

2. Siamese is to cat as _____ is to dog.
   wolf   collie   bark   Rover
   (A Siamese is a breed of cat.)

3. Cow is to herd as fish is to _____.
   school   fin   bunch   water
   (A group of cows is called a herd.)

4. Rooster is to hen as stallion is to _____.
   horse   mare   cow   rider
   (Roosters are male and hens are female.)

5. "Hoot" is to owl as "baa" is to _____.
   frog   chicken   sheep   goose
   (Owls make a noise that sounds like "hoot.")

Name _____   9

Animalogies II

Each numbered sentence is missing one word. Choose the word that *best* completes the sentence. Then write the word in the blank space. (If you need a hint, look at the statement below the sentence.)

1. Pack is to wolves as _____ is to birds.

   flock   school   flying   chirp

   (Wolves travel in packs.)

2. Cat is to kitten as bear is to _____.

   cub   baby   colt   honey

   (A cat is a mature kitten.)

3. Tadpole is to frog as caterpillar is to _____.

   insect   butterfly   cocoon   flight

   (A tadpole grows to become a frog.)

4. Insect is to bee as reptile is to _____.

   fish   crawling   snake   bat

   (A bee is a type of insect.)

5. Monkey is to jungle as camel is to _____.

   desert   humps   land   water

   (Monkeys live in the jungle.)

10   Name _____

Animalogies III

Complete the sentences below. First think carefully about the *relationship* of the words given. Then fill in the blank spaces with *two* words that have the same kind of *relationship.*

1. Colt is to horse as _____ is to _____ .

2. Herd is to cow as _____ is to _____ .

3. "Chirp" is to bird as _____ is to _____ .

4. Poodle is to dog as _____ is to _____ .

5. Dolphin is to ocean as _____ is to _____ .

6. Duck is to "quack" as _____ is to _____ .

7. Cow is to calf as _____ is to _____ .

8. Fish is to trout as _____ is to _____ .

9. Bird is to flock as _____ is to _____ .

10. Horse is to hay as _____ is to _____ .

11. Alligator is to reptile as _____ is to _____ .

12. Hen is to seed as _____ is to _____ .

Name _____

SEQUENCING

Even for children, it is important to learn how to organize events and things. By considering the steps involved in completing an activity, students can develop this natural skill.

Connect-the-Dots I and II: Students will perform the most basic sequencing skill—determining numerical order.

Pancake Flip Flop and Club Corner: Students will consider the steps in two common activities and will develop a plan based on the natural sequence of steps. A class discussion after one or both activities could begin by talking about why certain steps should be done before others.

Pizza Island, School Daze, and Family Reunion: Students will use spacial sequence skills with maps. In class discussion, students might describe their routes to school or exotic places. They could also discuss how a mode of transportation affects a travel route.

Showtime and Amusement Park: Students will plan a day's schedule. A class discussion could include problems of planning fun activities and schoolwork. The class could plan a fantasy adventure together.

Connect-the-Dots I

Connect the dots beside the numbers in order from 3 to 99. The numbers are multiples of *three.* The first line, from 3 to 6, has been drawn for you.

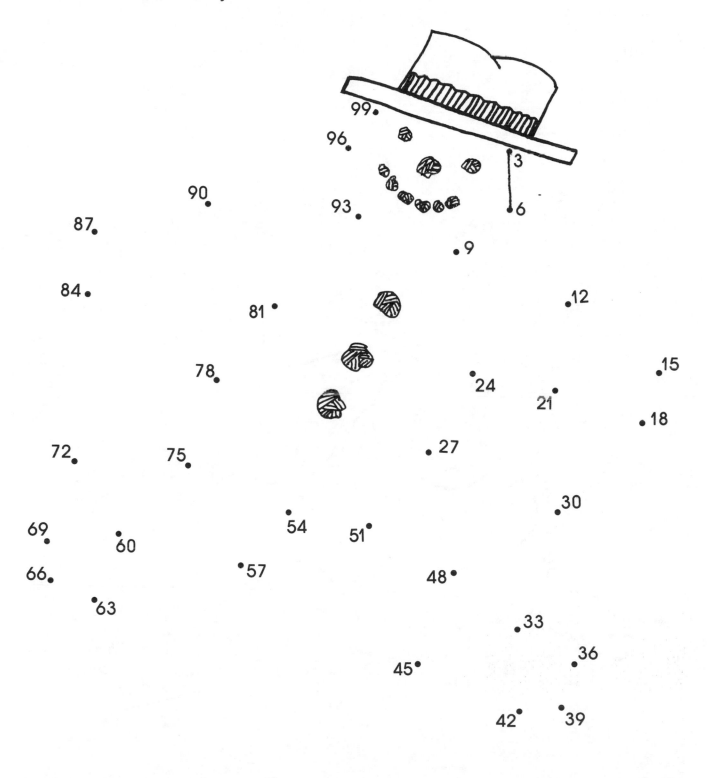

Connect-the-Dots II

Connect the dots beside the numbers in order from 4 to 112. The numbers are multiples of *four*. The first line, from 4 to 8, has been drawn for you.

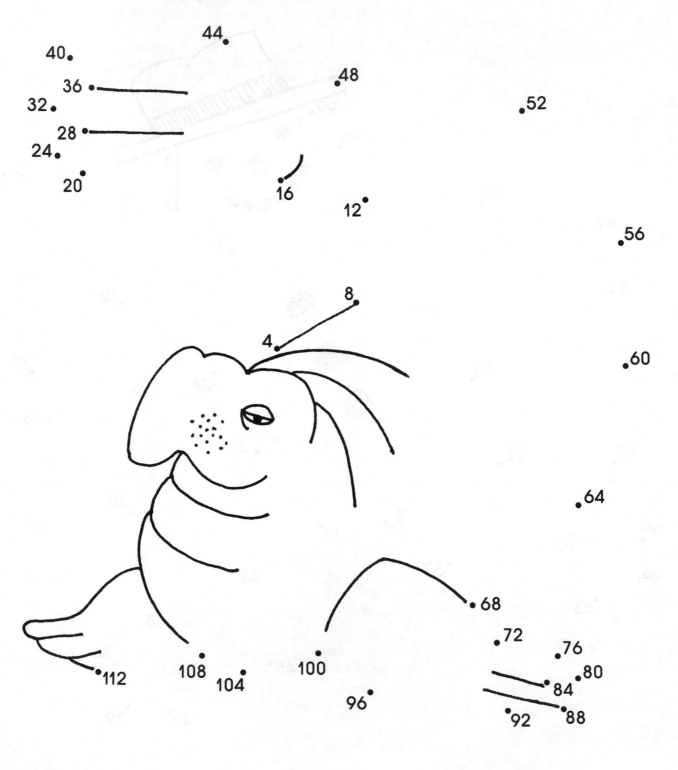

14   Name _____

Pancake Flip Flop

To make perfect pancakes you have to do everything in the right order. First think about making pancakes. Cross out *two* of the steps listed below that you don't need to make pancakes. Then number the steps 1 to 5 in the order they should be done.

Steps

a. _____ Mix the pancake batter while the skillet heats.

b. _____ Turn over the bacon.

c. _____ Pour the pancake batter into the hot skillet.

d. _____ Take out the ingredients for the pancake batter.

e. _____ Flip the pancakes to cook the other sides.

f. _____ Squeeze the oranges for juice.

g. _____ Serve the pancakes with syrup.

Name _____

Club Corner

Your club wants to make a clubhouse. Read the steps listed below. Then cross out the *two* steps that you do *not* need to complete the job. Then number the steps 1 to 6 in the order they should be done.

Steps

a. _____ Get the tools and the amount of wood needed for the design.

b. _____ Attach the roof to the walls.

c. _____ Elect the president of the club.

d. _____ Paint the clubhouse while it is still empty.

e. _____ Move in a table and some chairs.

f. _____ Put up the walls.

g. _____ Turn off the lights.

h. _____ Decide on a design for the clubhouse.

16   Name _____

Pizza Island

Two hundred years ago, Captain Pepperoni buried his treasure on Pizza Island. Then he drew a map with a path leading to the treasure. To keep his fortune secret, he cup up the map. His great-great-great-grandson Grayson found the pieces of the map in the attic. Grayson needs help putting the map back together. Cut out the pieces and arrange them so that the path leads from the rowboat to the treasure.

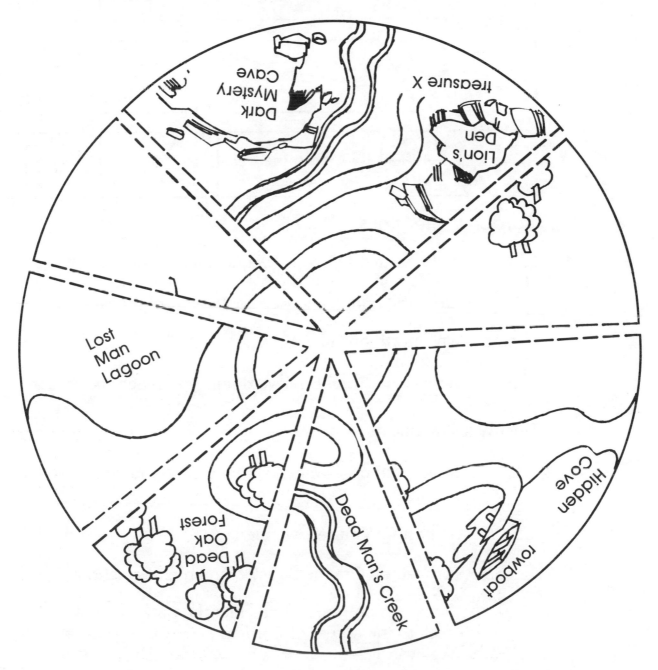

Name _____

School Daze

Gordon and Tiffany are going to school. Look at the map carefully. Then put the directions for going to school in order for each child by numbering the sentences 1, 2, 3, or 4.

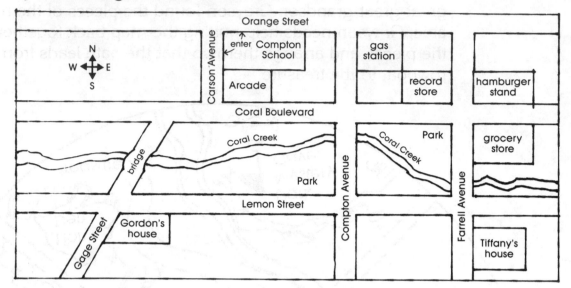

Gordon's Directions

_____ Walk north on Carson Avenue, then enter the school.

_____ Cross the bridge and walk to the end of the street.

_____ Walk north on Gage Street.

_____ Go east on Coral Boulevard until you reach the arcade.

Tiffany's Directions

_____ Walk north on Compton Avenue until you get to the gas station.

_____ Go north on Farrell Avenue.

_____ Turn left on Orange Street, then enter the school.

_____ Cross Lemon Street, then enter the park and follow the creek to the corner of Compton Avenue and Coral Boulevard.

Name _____

Family Reunion

The Brown family had a reunion in Green Bay, Wisconsin. Draw in the paths taken by Sharon's family and her cousin Henry's family.

Sharon and her family left Stockton Island. First they went to Lake Chippewa. Then they traveled along the Chippewa River, past Eau Claire, until they reached the Mississippi River. They drove directly across the state, crossing over two rivers, before reaching Green Bay.

Henry's family traveled to Green Bay from Platteville. First they went to Wisconsin's state capital, Madison. From there they went to the largest city on Lake Winnebago. They finished their trip by following the Fox River up to Green Bay.

Name _____

Showtime

You and your family are planning to spend the day at the Marine Park. There are four shows performed twice each day. Plan your schedule in the tour book at the bottom of the page so that you can see all four shows. The clock shows the starting time of each performance.

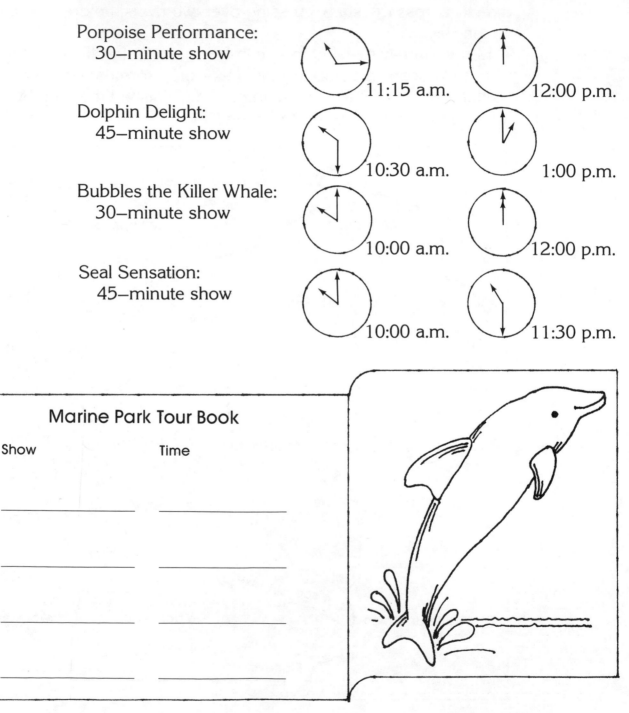

Porpoise Performance:
  30–minute show

Dolphin Delight:
  45–minute show

Bubbles the Killer Whale:
  30–minute show

Seal Sensation:
  45–minute show

11:15 a.m.   12:00 p.m.

10:30 a.m.   1:00 p.m.

10:00 a.m.   12:00 p.m.

10:00 a.m.   11:30 p.m.

Marine Park Tour Book

Show   Time

_____   _____

_____   _____

_____   _____

_____   _____

20   Name _____

Amusement Park

A few friends are having fun at the amusement park. They'd like to see all four shows. They also want to have at least an hour for lunch between 11:30 a.m. and 2:00 p.m. Plan a schedule for them and write it on the ticket packet, below. The clock shows the starting time for each performance.

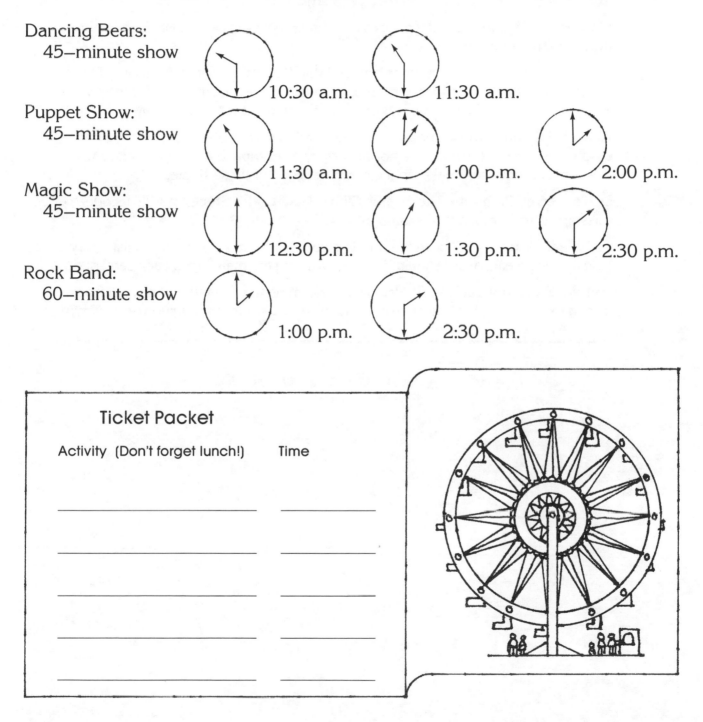

Dancing Bears:
45–minute show

10:30 a.m.   11:30 a.m.

Puppet Show:
45–minute show

11:30 a.m.   1:00 p.m.   2:00 p.m.

Magic Show:
45–minute show

12:30 p.m.   1:30 p.m.   2:30 p.m.

Rock Band:
60–minute show

1:00 p.m.   2:30 p.m.

Ticket Packet

Activity (Don't forget lunch!)   Time

_____   _____

_____   _____

_____   _____

_____   _____

Name _____   21

INFERENCE

Inference is the skill of reaching logical conclusions from gathered evidence. It is a deductive skill when the evidence is in the form of premises and an inductive skill when the evidence is in the form of specific examples. This section has examples of both types of inference problems.

Piece By Piece and Piece It Together: Students will visually reconstruct a picture from scrambled pieces.

Old Inventions—New Inventions and Holiday Match: Students will make inferences about new inventions that have replaced older inventions, and they will infer which United States holidays are like examples of foreign holidays.

Know It All? and Know Enough!: Students will decide what information is necessary and what information is not necessary to complete a task. For class discussion, students can make up their own versions of these riddles.

Lexi's Secret Club and The Secret Club's New Code: Students will decode a missing letter from a set of examples.

Tell-a-Pal: Students will fill in the missing words in a letter from a given list. They will infer where each word should go by determining the meaning of each sentence.

Pen Pal Problems I and II: Students will determine the meaning of a word from its context. This kind of inference helps to expand a student's reading vocabulary.

Piece By Piece

Look at the puzzle pieces below. Can you tell what animal the pieces can be arranged to make? Guess first, then cut out the pieces and put them together to see if you are right.

Name _____

Playing with Logic, copyright, © 1985 David S. Lake Publishers

Piece It Together

Look at the puzzle pieces below. Can you tell what object the pieces can be arranged to make? Guess first, then cut out the pieces and put them together to see if you are right.

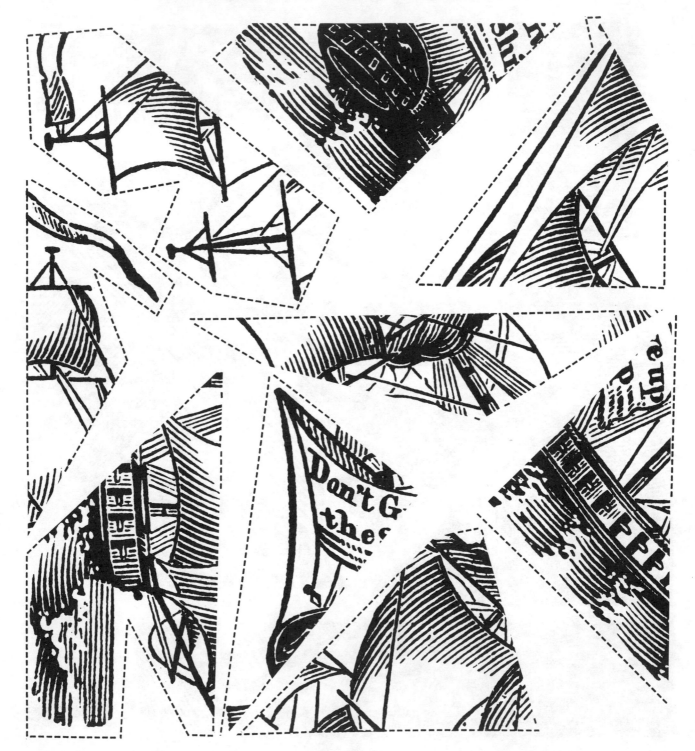

24   Name _____

Old Inventions—New Inventions

Most new inventions are improvements of old inventions. Below are descriptions and pictures of old inventions. At the bottom of the page is a list of some new inventions. Choose the name of the new invention that replaced the old one, and write it next to the picture.

Old Inventions

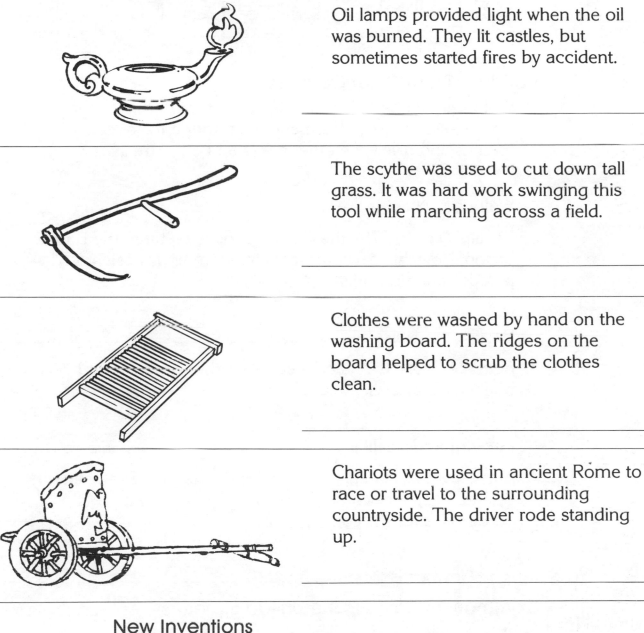

Oil lamps provided light when the oil was burned. They lit castles, but sometimes started fires by accident.

The scythe was used to cut down tall grass. It was hard work swinging this tool while marching across a field.

Clothes were washed by hand on the washing board. The ridges on the board helped to scrub the clothes clean.

Chariots were used in ancient Rome to race or travel to the surrounding countryside. The driver rode standing up.

New Inventions

automobile	washing machine	lawn mower
dishwasher	electric lamp	radio

Name _____

Holiday Match

Some countries celebrate holidays that are very much like our own. Read the description of each foreign holiday. Then complete each sentence with the United States holiday that is most like it. Choose from the list at the bottom of the page.

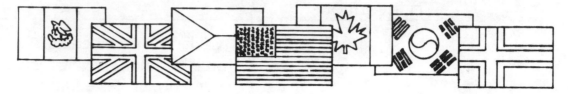

Holidays From Other Countries

1. Walpurgis Night: This is the night when witches play tricks and cast spells. People in Germany run through the streets with torches and give each other cakes and other treats.

   Walpurgis Night is like _____.

2. Bastille Day: In 1789 the French people captured the Bastille, a prison. Now this day represents freedom and is celebrated with parades and fireworks.

   Bastille day is like _____.

3. Feast of Fools: Long ago, people celebrated this feast by playing wild, clever pranks.

   Feast of Fools is like _____.

4. Aide Novrooz: In Iran, the calendar year begins on the first day of Spring. People celebrate this day and think about good possibilities for the coming year.

   Aide Novrooz is like _____.

Common Holidays in the United States

Fourth of July	Thanksgiving Day	Labor Day
Washington's Birthday	April Fools' Day	Halloween
Valentine's Day	New Year's Day	Memorial Day

26   Name _____

Know-It-All?

Sometimes you don't need to know it all. Below are four situations. For each one, cross out the item you don't need to know.

1. You are going to play in a baseball game. You need to know

    a. where the game will be played
    b. where you can get a ball and a bat
    c. what the score will be

2. You are going to bake a cake. You need to know

    a. what ingredients to use
    b. how long it takes to boil water
    c. what temperature the oven should be for the cake

3. You are going to fix a clock. You need to know

    a. what tools you need
    b. how a clock works
    c. what time the clock broke

4. You are going to build a birdhouse. You need to know

    a. what birds eat
    b. what materials are needed
    c. the size of the birds

Name _____   27

Playing with Logic, copyright, © 1985 David S. Lake Publishers

Know Enough!

It is enough to know enough! Below are four situations. For each one, cross out the item you do not need to know. Then, on the line below it, write something else you should know to complete the project.

1. You are acting in a play. You need to know

   a. what lines to speak

   b. who will be in the audience

   c. what props you need to hold

   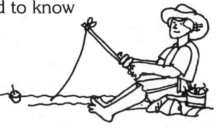

   d. _____

2. You are going trout fishing. You need to know

   a. what kind of bait to bring

   b. how to cook the fish

   c. which lakes have trout

   d. _____

3. You want to fly a kite. You need to know

   a. what color the kite is

   b. how to assemble the kite

   c. if there is enough wind to fly a kite

   d. _____

4. Your rock band is playing a concert. You need to know

   a. the name of the band that played last week

   b. what time to set up your equipment

   c. where the sockets are to plug in
      your instruments

   d. _____

Lexi's Secret Club

Discover the password to get into Lexi's secret club. In each set of words the same letter has been replaced by a shape. In the first set, the circle stands for "e." After you figure out the letter for each shape, fill in the password at the bottom of the page.

Set 1

to◯s

be◯t

cor◯

1◯ss

The ◯ stands for __e__ .

Set 2

△eat

li△e

lea△

△ice

The △ stands for _____ .

Set 3

ti◇e

rea◇

g◇ow

◇ast

The ◇ stands for _____ .

Set 4

b▢nd

co▢l

st▢r

mo▢n

The ▢ stands for _____ .

Set 5

▽ake

la▽e

▽ent

si▽k

The ▽ stands for _____ .

Set 6

◡are

co◡e

bea◡

◡ogs

The ◡ stands for _____ .

Password: _____ _____ _____ _____ _____ __e__
 ▽ ▢ △ ◡ ◇ ◯

The Secret Club's New Code

Lexi decided his club needs a new secret password, so he wrote a new code. Can you crack the code? In each set of words below, the same letter has been replaced by a shape. In the first set, the circle stands for "p." After you figure out the letters for each shape, fill in the password at the bottom of the page.

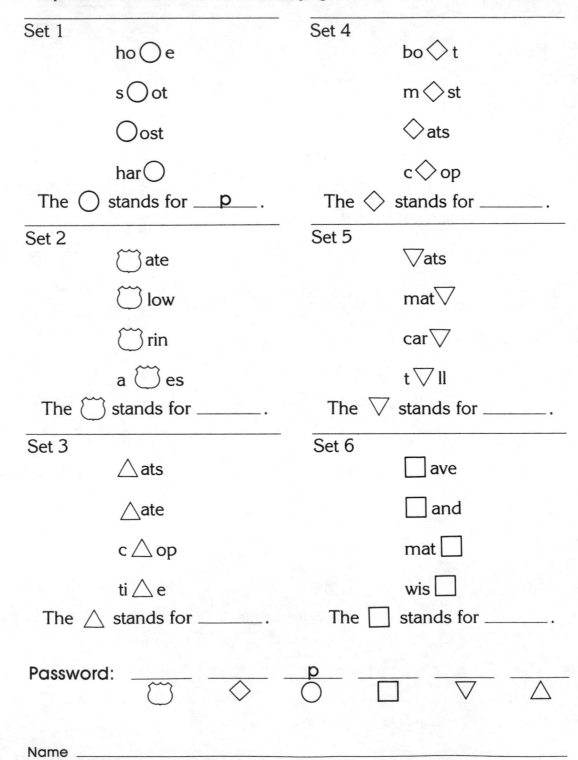

Set 1

ho◯e

s◯ot

◯ost

har◯

The ◯ stands for __p__ .

Set 2

⬭ate

⬭low

⬭rin

a⬭es

The ⬭ stands for _____ .

Set 3

△ats

△ate

c△op

ti△e

The △ stands for _____ .

Set 4

bo◇t

m◇st

◇ats

c◇op

The ◇ stands for _____ .

Set 5

▽ats

mat▽

car▽

t▽ll

The ▽ stands for _____ .

Set 6

☐ave

☐and

mat☐

wis☐

The ☐ stands for _____ .

Password: ___ ___ _p_ ___ ___ ___
⬭   ◇   ◯   ☐   ▽   △

30   Name _____

Tell-A-Pal

In a letter to Svens, your pen pal in Denmark, you describe a parade. Use the words listed below in the letter. Write each word on the blank line in the letter where it fits best. Use each word only once.

crowd	tow truck	letter	music	floats	sandwiches
parade	parents	clowns	mother	tuba	popcorn

Dear Svens,

Thank you for your last _____ . This last New Year's Day,

my _____ took us to see a _____ on Main Street. There were

animals, _____ , and many pretty _____ with flowers. One was

being pulled by a car that broke down. A _____ came and took it

away. The whole _____ cheered when the parade began moving again.

Next, we saw a marching band that played wonderful _____ .

My _____ told us she used to play the _____ in a marching

band. The whole time we watched we were eating _____ , so later

when my dad gave us chicken _____ we weren't hungry. We had lots

of fun, and I hope when you come to visit you can see a parade.

Sincerely,

Name _____

Pen Pal Problems I

Lisa has a pen pal in Russia. Kevin's pen pal is from Japan, and Stacy's pen pal lives in Israel. They received letters written in English but each letter has a foreign word in it. Read each letter and figure out the meaning of its mysterious word. Then write the word below the letter.

Dear Lisa,

It is good that my mother keeps many extra _____CBEYEK_____ in the cupboard. (I don't know the English word for _____CBEYEK_____.) Last night, during a storm, all the electricity went off. We set up _____CBEYEK_____ all over the house. I used a match to light them and the glow was pretty.

    I must go now, Uri

The Russian word _____CBEYEK_____ means _____.

Dear Kevin,

I have been reading a lot—not only books but the _____新聞(紙)_____.
(How do you say it in English?) I follow our baseball scores, and I read about what is happening in Tokyo, our capital. Does your _____新聞(紙)_____ have weather reports?

        Love, Atsuo

The Japanese word _____新聞(紙)_____ means _____.

Dear Stacy,

We have cucumbers and lemons in our _____גנה_____. (What's the English word? I don't know.) Soon the fruits and vegetables will be ready to eat, and I will get to pick them. Keeping a _____גנה_____ in Haifa is difficult because it needs to be watered often.

        Your friend, Dvora

The Hebrew word _____גנה_____ means _____.

Pen Pal Problems II

Josh and Diane just received letters from their pen pals, but each letter has two or three foreign words in it. Read each letter and figure out the meanings of the foreign words. Then write the meanings in the spaces provided.

Dear Josh,

Until last Sunday, I had never been to a __馬戲場__. (I don't know the word in English.) There were large tents filled with animals doing tricks and gymnasts swinging on bars. My favorite character at the __馬戲場__ was the __小丑兒__. (Another new word!) He had a big smile painted on his face but he didn't look very happy. He kept falling down and another __小丑兒__ played funny tricks on him.

Your friend, Peying

The Chinese word __馬戲場__ means _____,

and the word __小丑兒__ means _____.

Dear Diane,

For my birthday, I got a __دوربین یا جیبعكاسی__ (English?) My mother showed me how to use it the same day. At my party, I used a whole roll of __پردهٔ نازك__. (Sorry, I do not know the English word.) There is a funny __عكس__ (sorry again) of my dad carrying in the cake and another one of my little sister spilling her piece. If you have a __عكس__ of yourself, I would like to see it. Maybe your brother has a __دوربین یا جیبعكاسی__ to take one. It would be wonderful if he used color __پردهٔ نازك__. I must go now.

Sincerely, Fariba

The Farsi word __دوربین یا جیبعكاسی__ means _____,

the word __پردهٔ نازك__ means _____,

and the word __عكس__ means _____.

Playing with Logic, copyright, © 1985 David S. Lake Publishers

DEDUCTION

Techniques such as process of elimination, trial and error, and combining clues are required to solve these riddle-like problems. The problems start out simple and get progressively more difficult.

Rainbow Duck Walk, Rainbow Ducks Go Swimming, Grandma Annie's Farm, and Water Ways: Students will deduce the position of objects from direct clues.

The Juggling Clown, Ferris Wheel, Seal Show, Halloween Hats, Leash Work, Cool Collar Colors, and Birthday Party: Students will solve riddles that require them to combine and reorganize clues.

Three-on-Three, Video Wiz, Video Master, and House Painting: Students will solve problems that involve numbers or less direct clue combinations. You might consider using these puzzles in a group activity. Those students who have not developed effective puzzle solving strategies can learn from the strategies of other students.

Rainbow Duck Walk

The Rainbow Ducks are out for a walk. Read the clues and write the correct name under each duck.

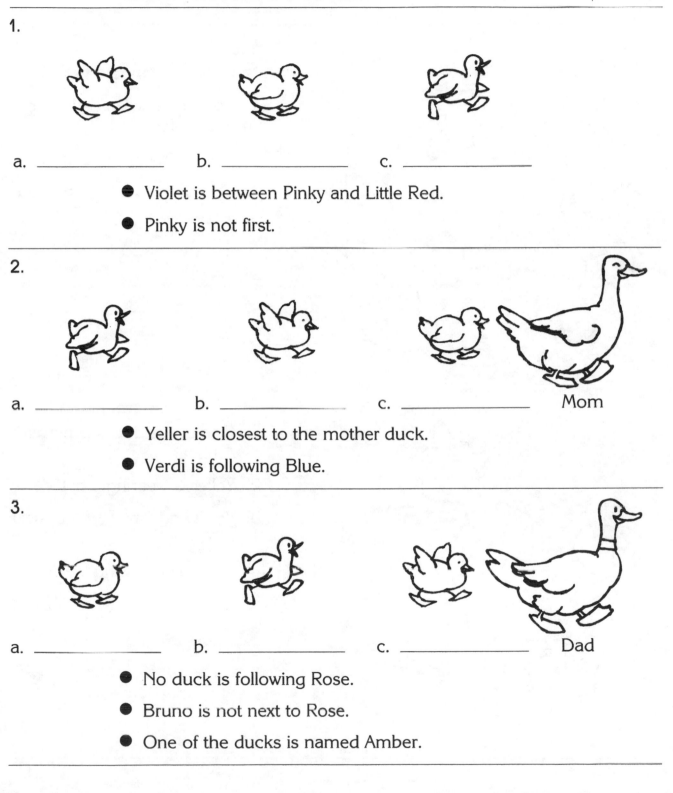

1.

a. _____ b. _____ c. _____

- Violet is between Pinky and Little Red.
- Pinky is not first.

2.

a. _____ b. _____ c. _____ Mom

- Yeller is closest to the mother duck.
- Verdi is following Blue.

3.

a. _____ b. _____ c. _____ Dad

- No duck is following Rose.
- Bruno is not next to Rose.
- One of the ducks is named Amber.

Name _____ 35

Rainbow Ducks Go Swimming

The Rainbow Ducks are swimming in the pond. Read all the clues carefully. Then write the correct name next to each duck.

Clues

1. Rose is wearing a hat.

2. Rose is between Little Red and Violet.

3. Violet is following Bruno.

4. One of the ducks is named Blue.

1. One of the ducks is named Amber.

2. Yeller is wearing a hat.

3. Verdi and Pinky are not next to Yeller.

4. Goldy is following Verdi.

Playing with Logic, copyright, © 1985 David S. Lake Publishers

Grandma Annie's Farm

Four cousins visited Grandma Annie's Farm. They each had one chore:

Rani milked the cows.

Jeffrey groomed the horses.

Brian fed the chickens.

Rachel collected chicken eggs.

One day they all switched to different chores. Read the clues below. Then put X's in the grid to match each person's name with the new chore.

Clues

1. Rani wanted the chore that Jeffrey did before.

2. Jeffrey took the chore left over after everyone else chose a new chore.

3. Brian's new chore was with the same animals as was his old chore.

4. Rachel was worried that she might spill the milk, but she thought she would give it a try.

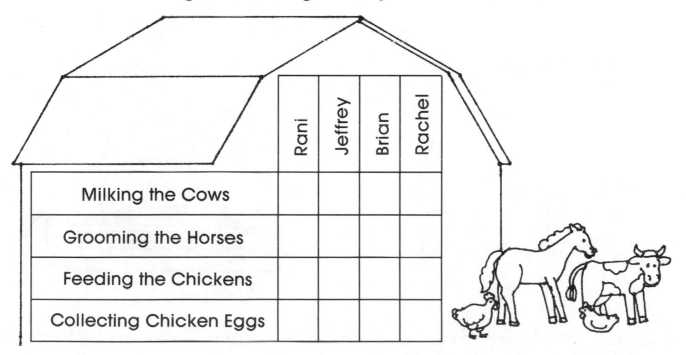

Playing with Logic, copyright, © 1985 David S. Lake Publishers

Water Ways

Four brothers and sisters—Debbie, John, Jerry, and Bonnie—all like to play in different bodies of water. Read the clues below. Then, in the blank below each body of water, write the name of the person who likes it most.

Clues

1. John doesn't like to swim where fish may be in the water.

2. Debbie dislikes river rafting even though it is her sister's favorite sport.

3. Debbie's favorite sport is deep sea fishing.

4. Jerry water skis in Lake Arrow every chance he gets.

a. _____
Atlantic Ocean

b. _____
Moon River

c. _____
Lake Arrow

d. _____
Community Swimming Pool

The Juggling Clown

The clown is too busy juggling to color in the balls. Help the clown.
Read the clues, then write the correct color next to each ball.

Clues

1. One of the balls is purple.

2. The red ball is between the juggler's hands.

3. The green ball is highest.

4. The blue ball is not next to the green one.

5. The yellow ball is between the blue and green ones.

Ferris Wheel

Seven friends are riding the Ferris wheel at the carnival. Read the clues to help you decide who is riding in each car. Then write the riders' names on the cars.

Clues

1. The Ferris wheel is moving clockwise (in the direction of the arrows).

2. Lester is in the lowest car moving upwards.

3. Cindy, in the highest car, has the best view of the city.

4. Shana is between Calvin and Ellen.

5. Cindy is between two boys. Henry is one of them.

6. Put Terri's name on her car.

Boys
Lester, Calvin, Henry

Girls
Cindy, Shana, Ellen, Terri

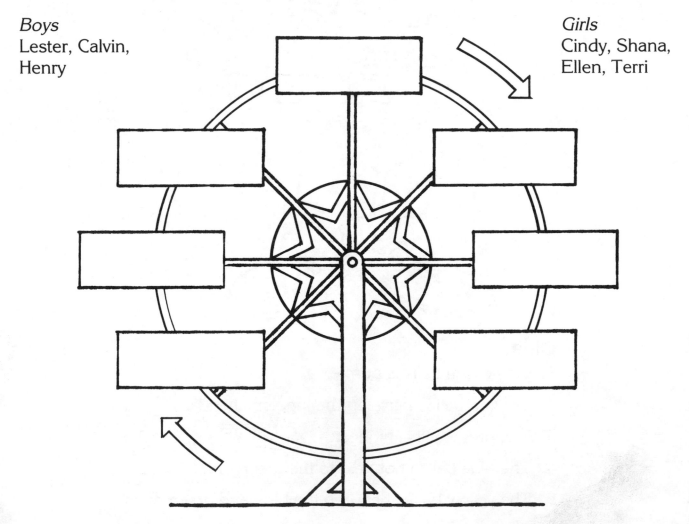

Name _____

Seal Show

Five seals are balancing objects on their noses. Read the clues below. Then write the name of each seal on the line underneath the stand.

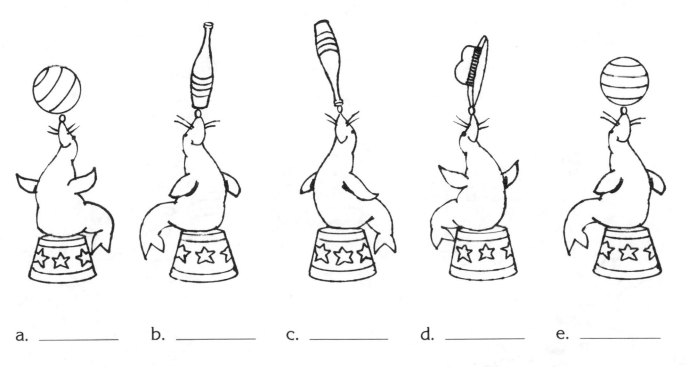

a. _____ b. _____ c. _____ d. _____ e. _____

Clues

1. Topo, who is next to Akbar, is on one end balancing a ball on his nose.

2. Evita, who is between Doris and Akbar, is balancing a pin on her nose.

3. Nikko is balancing a ball and is next to a seal who is balancing a pin.

Name _____

Playing with Logic, copyright, © 1985 David S. Lake Publishers

Halloween Hats

Five friends dressed up for a Halloween party. In all, there was one witch, one pirate, one firefighter, one sailor, and one chef at the party. Read the clues below. Then, on the line nearest each person, write the costume he or she wore.

b. _____ c. _____ d. _____

a. _____   e. _____

Clues

1. The pirate is sitting at one end of the table, and his sister, the sailor, is sitting at the other end.

2. The chef is not next to the firefighter.

3. The firefighter is next to her best friend, the pirate.

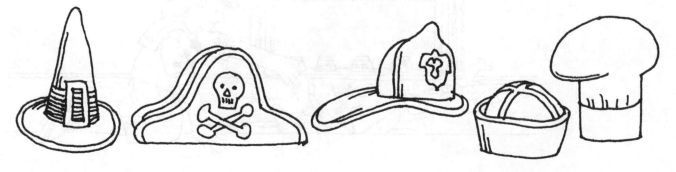

Name _____

Leash Work

Four friends walked their dogs in the park. Read the clues below. Then, put X's in the grid to match each dog with the correct owner.

	Sally	Jim	Andy	Natalie
Poodle				
Saint Bernard				
German Shepherd				
Bulldog				

Clues

1. Sally and Jim often take their dogs, the poodle and the bulldog, for walks together.

2. Jim and Andy decided to get watchdogs. One of them chose a German shepherd.

3. Sally bought matching bows for her hair and for her poodle.

4. Natalie likes Saint Bernards and German shepherds. She owns one of the two.

Name _____

Cool Collar Colors

Each dog's collar is a different color. Read the clues at the bottom of the page. Then put X's in the grid below to match the owners' names with the correct colors.

Bonnie

	Red	Orange	Green	Blue
Bonnie				
Greg				
Oliver				
Robin				

Greg   Oliver   Robin

Clues

1. The color of each dog's collar begins with a letter that is *different* from the first letter of the owner's name.

2. Greg and Bonnie won't buy anything red for their red-haired Irish setters.

3. Oliver bought a red collar for his dog.

4. Bonnie's dog does not have a green collar.

Birthday Party

At Jamie's eighth birthday party, each of his four guests gave him a different gift, and each won a different party game. Read the clues below and write the correct gifts and games under each person's name.

Guests	Carol	Melanie	Hans	Amy
Gifts				
Games				

Clues

Gifts

1. Carol knitted the sweater she gave Jamie.

2. Someone brought a 250-piece jigsaw puzzle.

3. Both Carol and Hans wanted to bring a video game. Only one of them did.

4. The record that Amy gave was Jamie's favorite gift.

Party Games Winners

1. Melanie, the best guesser, won the game of "twenty questions."

2. Carol and the girl who won "musical chairs" are best friends.

3. The girl who brought the sweater did not win at "hide-and-seek."

4. The treasure hunt was the most exciting game.

Name _____

Playing with Logic, copyright, © 1985 David S. Lake Publishers

Three-on-Three

The blue team and the red team played basketball. Everyone's uniform had a different number. Their numbers are listed below. Use the clues at the bottom of the page to figure out which number to write on each player's uniform.

3   4   8   9   16   17

The Red Team   The Blue Team

Clues

1. Everyone on the red team has an even number.

2. The tallest player has the highest number *on his team.*

3. The two shortest players are wearing the lowest numbers.

4. The tallest player on the blue team does not have the highest number on his team.

Video Wiz

The school cafeteria got a new video game. After the first lunch period, the five highest scores were displayed. Using the clues below, fill in the initials of the person who earned each score.

Clues

1. Angie York scored highest.

2. Harley Kender scored 10,000 points lower than Angie.

3. Phil Rogers did not score higher than Harley.

4. Linda Wells scored higher than Harley but lower than Greg Owens.

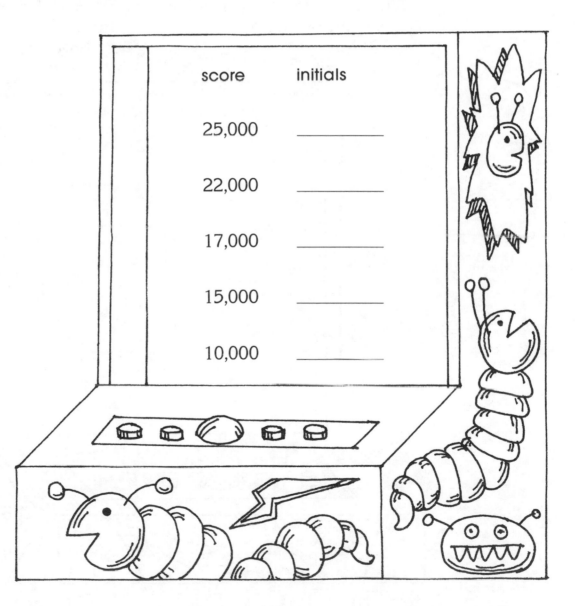

score	initials
25,000	_____
22,000	_____
17,000	_____
15,000	_____
10,000	_____

Name _____

Video Master

Five friends played the video game "Spider Web." At the end of the game, the computer displayed their initials in order of most points earned, with the highest score on top. Using the clues below, write the correct score next to each person's initials.

Clues

1. Larry Edwards was upset that he scored only 41,000 points.

2. Michelle Lane scored 4,000 points more than Nicole Adams.

3. Ron Williams usually scores better than the 45,000 points he earned in this game.

4. Florence Lewis scored 1,000 points more than Michelle's score of 48,000.

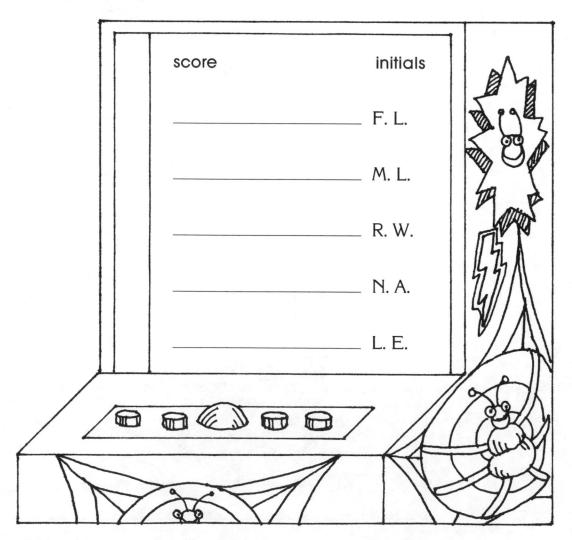

score   initials

_____ F. L.

_____ M. L.

_____ R. W.

_____ N. A.

_____ L. E.

Name _____

House Painting

The members of a camping club painted the first floor of a friend's house to earn some money for their club. Each person painted a different room, and each room was painted a different color. Using the clues below, put X's in the grid to match the room and the color to each painter.

	Living Room	Dining Room	Kitchen	Work Room	Den	Green	Red	Brown	Yellow	Blue
Valerie										
Roy										
Jodi										
Helen										
Lucky										

Clues

1. Valerie painted the room farthest from the kitchen.

2. The room that Roy painted had doors which led directly into every other room except the room where Jodi painted.

3. Helen did not paint the dining room.

4. Lucky was spattered with red paint from the room he painted.

5. When Valerie left her room with her paintbrush, she tried not to get green paint on the fresh blue paint of the living room.

6. Jodi wore yellow overalls to match the room she painted.

7. One of the rooms was painted brown.

GROUP ACTIVITIES

The games in this section are designed to provide practice in the skills developed throughout the previous four sections (Relationships, Sequencing, Inference, and Deduction).

All of the games involve following directions and cooperating with fellow students. Each game reinforces logical skills. At the beginning of each game is a description of the object of the game, the group size the game is designed for, any materials required to play the game, preparations for playing the game, and a description of how the game is played. Some activity pages offer variations of the basic game rules.

The following are suggestions on the section that each game should accompany.

Match-Up: Relationships or Sequencing

Because, Because: Sequencing

Word Around: Inference

Fable Stable: Inference or Deduction

Match-Up

Object: To develop visual or tactile discrimination, negative and positive shape concepts, and classification skills.

Group size: Five students or less per group.

Materials: One piece of construction paper per student; crayons; and scissors.

Preparation: Give each student a sheet of construction paper and a crayon. Have students fold the paper in half and draw a geometric design along the folded edge. Within each group, no duplicate drawings should be made. Have the students cut out the shapes. They will then have a cut-out shape and the original folded paper with a negative of that shape.

Sample drawings:

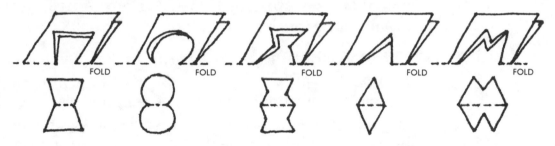

How to Play

1. Choose one member of each group to collect all the cut-out shapes. That person will be the player for the first round.

2. Have the rest of the group form a circle around the player and have each student place the paper "negative" of a shape, unfolded, in front of them.

3. Instruct the player to visualize which negative each shape fits, then place each shape in the correct negative.

4. Then choose a new player for each group and repeat the round.

5. After two or three rounds, each group will become familiar with its shapes, so have the groups exchange sets of shapes and negatives.

Variation: To make the game more challenging, the players can hold the shapes behind their backs so that they must use their sense of touch to match the shapes.

Because, Because

Object: Players compose a plausible chain of reasoning.

Group size: Five to twenty students.

Preparation: Arrange the students in a circle.

How to Play

1. Instruct a player to begin by stating a simple sentence. (Or you may want to begin the first round.)

2. Have the next player repeat the sentence and add a "because" clause to explain the sentence. For example, it the first player said, "I am hungry," the second player might say, "I am hungry because I had no breakfast."

3. Have the next player make the new clause the main clause and invent another "because" clause. For example: "I had no breakfast because I got up late."

4. The story continues until a player makes an illogical connection or repeats a phrase. Then a new round may be started. Note: Although the students should be responsible for pointing out illogical connections, you may want to give an example. For example: "I had no breakfast because I am hungry."

Variation: To emphasize narrative sequencing rather than causal relationships, instead of using "because," have the students say "after that," and then add a logical connecting sentence.

Word Around

Object: Students change only one element of a whole word.

Group Size: Five to seven students.

Preparation: Seat each group in a circle. Select one person to be the recorder for the first round.

How to Play

1. Have one player begin by spelling a three, four, or five letter word. (You should decide ahead of time how many letters the words will have, and you may vary the amount for other rounds.) The recorder, who also participates, writes that word and subsequent words.

2. Instruct the next player to say and spell a word that is identical to the first word except for one letter. For example, the first player might say "hand" and the next player might say "land," "hind," or "hard."

3. Have each player around the circle continue to transform the word, one letter at a time, in turn.

4. If a person repeats, misspells, or changes a word by two or more letters, that person becomes the recorder for a new round. The next player in the circle begins the new round by saying a new word.

Variations: You may give a list of starting words. Good starters include: day, cry, him, lot, bed, game, hand, tire, first, and born.

Fable Stable

Object: Players match fables to morals.

Group Size: Ten groups of two, three, or four students.

Preparation: Make ten copies of the "Fable Morals" list on the following page. On each list, circle a different moral. Give each group a list.

How to Play

1. Instruct each group to plan a skit that will illustrate the moral that is circled on their list. They may use fables they know or make up their own. Monitor the progress of each group and offer help when it is needed.

2. Each group presents its skit to the class in turn.

3. The students in each group decide which fables were illustrated by each of the skits.

4. Each group presents its results to the class.

5. Any differences between the groups' results are discussed.

Variation: You do not need to use all of the morals. In a class of twenty-four, for example, there may be six groups of four students. Then, only six morals will be circled and the students will guess from among the entire list of ten morals.

Fable Morals

Sometimes, being quiet is the best reply.

Two people working together are better than three working alone.

Even when telling the truth, a liar is not to be believed.

It's not how much, but how good that counts.

If you want a job done your way, you must do it yourself.

A person who eats the fruit he can reach won't be as hungry as one who watches the fruit beyond his reach.

Don't be surprised if your are treated the way you treat others.

Not even a thief can trust a thief.

You might fool a wise person with a trick once, but not twice.

Sometimes it is luckier to be small than to be large.

ANSWER KEY

RELATIONSHIPS

Make a Set I

(cross out)	(fill in)
1. bugle	in a kitchen
2. snowshoes	at the beach
3. bowl	in a toolbox
4. bathtub	at a school

Make a Set II

(cross out)	(fill in)
1. jump rope	for making music
2. flagpole	for playing
3. tennis net	for baseball
4. camera	for traveling

The Zoo on Planet Woo

1. Scoo Frooch	2. Frooch
3. Scoo Ploom	4. Ploom
5. Scoo	6. Frooch Ploom
7. Frooch	8. Scoo Frooch

Creatures of the Lost Island

1. Arachnid	2. Anura	3. Mammal
4. "X"	5. Arachnid	6. Anura
7. Anura	8. Mammal	9. Arachnid

Shapes Alike

1. c   2. b   3. a   4. b   5. b

Shapes Relate

1. c   2. d   3. b   4. a   5. a

Animalogies I

1. dog	2. collie	3. school
4. mare	5. sheep	

Animalogies II

1. flock	2. cub	3. butterfly
4. snake	5. desert	

Animalogies III (possible solutions)

1. kitten—cat	2. flock—birds
3. "moo"—cow	4. parakeet—bird
5. lizard—desert	6. frog—"ribbit"
7. ewe—lamb	8. bird—robin
9. buffalo—herd	10. rabbit—lettuce
11. whale—mammal	12. cow—grass

SEQUENCING

Pancake Flip Flop

a. 2   b. X   c. 3   d. 1
e. 4   f. X   g. 5

Club Corner

a. 2   b. 4   c. X   d. 5
e. 6   f. 3   g. X   h. 1

Pizza Island

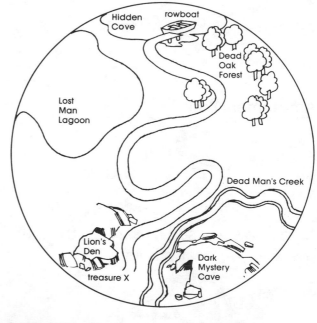

School Daze

Gordon: 4, 2, 1, 3
Tiffany: 3, 1, 4, 2

ANSWER KEY

Family Reunion

Showtime

Seal Show	10:00
Porpoise Show	11:15
Whale Show	12:00
Dolphin Show	1:00

Amusement Park

Dancing Bears	10:30
Puppet Show	11:30
lunch	12:15
Magic Show	1:30
Rock Band	2:30

INFERENCE

Piece By Piece

A lion

Piece It Together

A sailboat

Old Inventions—New Inventions

1. light bulb
2. lawn mower
3. washing machine
4. automobile

Holiday Match

1. Halloween
2. Fourth of July
3. April Fools' Day
4. New Year's Day

Know It All?

(cross out)

1. what the score will be.
2. how long it takes to boil water.
3. what time the clock broke.
4. what birds eat.

Know Enough?

(cross out)

1. who will be in the audience.
2. how to cook the fish.
3. what color the kite is.
4. the name of the band that played last week.

(possible fill in)

1. when to come on stage.
2. where is your fishing reel.
3. how to get the kite in the air.
4. how much money you will earn.

Lexi's Secret Club

c a n d l e

Secret Club's New Code

g o p h e r

Tell-A-Pal

letter, parents, parade, clowns, floats, tow truck, crowd, music, mother, tuba, popcorn, sandwiches

Pen Pal Problems I

Lisa: candles   Kevin: newspaper
Stacy: garden

ANSWER KEY

Pen Pal Problems II

Josh: circus, clown
Diane: camera, film, photograph

DEDUCTION

Rainbow Duck Walk

1. a. Little Red   b. Violet   c. Pinky
2. a. Verdi   b. Blue   c. Yeller
3. a. Rose   b. Amber   c. Bruno

Rainbow Ducks Go Swimming

1.

2.

Grandma Annie's Farm

Rani groomed the horses.
Jeffrey fed the chickens.
Brian collected chicken eggs.
Rachel milked the cows.

Water Ways

a. Debbie   b. Bonnie
c. Jerry   d. John

The Juggling Clown

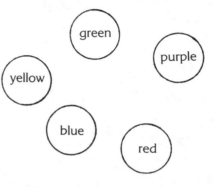

Ferris Wheel

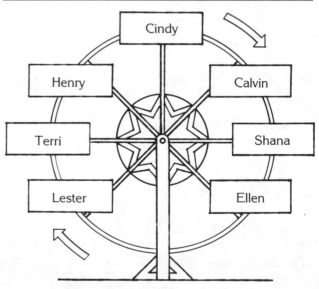

ANSWER KEY

Seal Show

a. Nikko   b. Doris   c. Evita
    d. Akbar   e. Topo

Halloween Hats

pirate—firefighter—witch—chef—sailor

Leash Work

Jim: bulldog   Andy: German shepherd
Natalie: Saint Bernard   Sally: poodle

Cool Collar Colors

Bonnie: orange   Greg: blue
Oliver: red   Robin: green

Birthday Party

	Carol	Melanie	Hans	Amy
Gifts:	sweater	puzzle	video game	record
Games:	treasure hunt	twenty questions	hide-and-seek	musical chairs

Three-on-Three

Red Team: 8–16–4
Blue Team: 17—3—9

Video Wiz

A. Y.	25,000
G. O.	22,000
L. W.	17,000
H. K.	15,000
P. R.	10,000

Video Master

F. L.	49,000
M. L.	48,000
R. W.	45,000
N. A.	44,000
L. E.	41,000

House Painting

Valerie: workroom—green
Roy: living room—blue
Jodi: kitchen—yellow
Helen: den—brown
Lucky: dining room—red